SUNDAY NIGHT MARGARITA-FUELED SHOUT-OUTS
BORROWED WISDOM & COLLECTED BEAUTY

**75 JOURNAL PROMPTS FROM
A PARK BENCH OBSERVER**

KELLEY ROSE

Copyright © 2018

ISBN: 1544820097

To unexpected angels and the
lessons they continue to teach.

This book is a tribute to a hard-candy shell of
a man who died way too young.

**It is also a beating drum plea for the
use of sunscreen every single day.**

A portion of all book sales go toward
finding a cure for melanoma.

SIT BESIDE THE ONE WHO SMILES WITH THEIR EYES FIRST

THERE'S A STORY THERE

When my dad was sick - really sick, he seemed different. Not just physically, but mentally. Unlike ever before, he was more sentimental and more in-tune with the emotions of others around him. I found myself wondering many times if this might be common for those fully understanding that the end of their life was near.

He hugged a lot more and laughed a little louder than I had ever remembered him doing. He seemed to know something that the rest of us just couldn't or wouldn't allow ourselves yet to know. Glancing back, I now understand the urgency and uncharacteristic presence he had. I've come to view this transition from life to death as beautiful….as strangely as that seems. At fourteen though, I just wasn't quite there.

My dad was one of those **really complex, enigma-like sort of people**. Everything he did was overdone, complicated and epic. He could take the simplest of concepts and mangle it until you had a headache. He was smart though and he was never hesitant in letting that be known. Dad was only six feet but always seemed like the tallest guy in the room. His energy was palpable and sometimes even overbearing. He was a staunch conservative. I was once told that one of the names my parents had considered using was Reagan. You know, after Ronald.

His cooking was legendary. I don't really remember him ever having to go to the store for ingredients. He'd normally just look in the fridge and come up with something sublime. It was one of the few things I remember him never having to try to be good at. I don't mean to say he wasn't good at lots of things, he most certainly was. But more often than not, **he worked his ass off for his signature results.** Dad was no stranger to hard work.

He was the sole inventor of the infamous Birthday Pancake Cake. To clarify to all those who have not yet been on the receiving end of such a masterpiece, it was a stack of seven medium-sized pancakes. Why seven?

"Because it is the perfect height and can hold the weight of the icing, Jess," he once explained with the confidence of a man who had obviously used trial and error to delight us.

Birthday Pancake Cakes were custom-made to their giftees' specific preference and favorite flavors. Mine was dark chocolate and strawberries covered in homemade whipped cream. Every year he'd put a different spin on it. I'll never forget the last one he made. It was for my little brother. Dad was so sick he could barely get out of bed but there was absolutely no way he was going to let his kid go pancake-less on his birthday. It was seven microwaved pancakes pathetically slapped together with some icing from a can with a single candle on top…and it turned out to be the most perfect Birthday Pancake Cake he'd ever made.

He loved his job. He worked as a pharmaceutical sales rep. He'd make me watch these gruesome neurological surgeries that he'd been able to sit in on and had somehow gotten bootleg films of. They lasted hours and bored me to tears. He'd explain every single step and and remind me every time how he'd had to tell the attending physicians where to put the drug inside the patient's brain. He made me go through these flashcards that were typically reserved for fourth year med students and insisted I learn about the different parasites that can worm their way into a human. Yes, he really *really* wanted me to be a doctor.

Dad was loud and he never hesitated to inform you in high decibels when you disappointed him. He definitely wasn't the type to generally back down from a fight. He'd usually keep goading us until we'd get so annoyed we'd leave in a huff barely remembering the subject of the discussion. And when you did, he'd usually laugh. Or make up a song. TO THIS DAY I am physically unable to listen to the song "Stop and Stare" without getting a strange combination of anger and laughter at the memory of his "Stomp and Storm" rendition for whenever I briskly exited a room.

He was a handyman. Kind of. You could always find him outside with sawdust piles of varying heights surrounding him. He insisted on wearing a purple, polka-dotted, scrub hat in the middle of the Texas heat while crafting his latest project. I remember being mortified to find him like that on several occasions with my friends in tow. I tried to explain how embarrassing he was, but do you think he was bothered for even half a second?

He loved golf, both watching and playing. And though he'd mastered the art of watching, he was seriously horrible at the playing part. He was a club-throwing, cursing, menace on the green. I went with him a few times when I was younger and wished myself to be anywhere but there. It felt like a good walk spoiled most certainly. He was unfazed.

He was, in the most over-simplified generalization, a true lover and a fighter. He exuded passion in just about everything (even if he wasn't that great at it) and he stood up for what he thought was right (even if it really wasn't).

I could continue to describe the incredible intricacies of the man I was honored to call my dad for fourteen years, but the truth is, those memories are really only that special and interesting to *me*. And that has been the hardest part of losing him-the inability to convey his absolute complexity alongside the beauty and magic he left us to anyone that never got the chance to know him. The second hardest thing, is not knowing what he'd think of me. Would he hate that I didn't grow up to be a conservative like him? Would he be disappointed I chose law school over medical school? Would he shake his head due to the fact that I simply can't seem to rid myself of the self-deprecating, cynical, sarcastic humor? Would he like me? Those questions seem so easy for others to answer. "Of course! He'd be so proud of you, you know that!" And I guess they're right. But it would be so much better coming from him.

I was a swimmer growing up. More like a pool rat. I think my parents loved it more than me but I was decent so I kept at it. They would scream their lungs out at my meets. I still have dreams where I can hear them yelling "Pull!" every time I come up for a breath. I swam all the way up until my freshman year of high school. Dad was in the midst of chemo and starting to get really weak. Shamefully, I remember being embarrassed when he showed up to one of my meets looking so frail and bald. There was one day, however, where my teenaged bratty brain actually came in handy. As I mentioned, Dad was incredibly emotional toward the end. For the most part, it was this weird sappiness. Other times, it was fear. Which I did not understand. My dad didn't cry. He wasn't supposed to be scared of things.

One day, as he was about to leave for chemo, he broke down in complete tears—a full on meltdown. He doesn't want to go, he said. He can't do it again, he cried.

I snapped.

"Dad! Shut up! You have to go. Just do it! Stop hugging me and go get in the damn car!"

He looked broken. But he just walked outside and got into the car. I don't remember how I felt immediately after that exchange. But I'll never forget how I felt when he came back. He sat down on the couch and just stared at me.

"Thank you," he whispered.

I sat across from him and just nodded my head. I wanted him to know that I loved him and just wanted him to go to chemo because at that point I was convinced it would work. But for some reason those words didn't come out.

Instead I said, **"You just have to touch the wall, Dad."**

"It's like swimming, I explained. Sometimes I'm in that pool during a meet and it feels like I'll die if I have to swim one more lap. But I just keep telling myself to touch the wall, to get to the other side of the pool and I'm done."

He smiled and said, "Okay, I'll touch the wall."

And *touch the wall* he kept doing until it was his time to go. He left me and my siblings and mom in good hands with many people who will love us for the rest of our lives. He didn't choose any cookie cutter meek or mild people to watch over us all, instead he spent the last part of his life preparing a few hand-picked characters to crack the whip and help shape us into individual thinkers full of curiosity and dedicated to service. He chose those who would embolden us to be exactly who we were becoming. He picked people who loved him for who he was and were committed to reminding us of his essence and mark on life without granting him sainthood, hindsight. He choose those who would would keep him alive in our hearts forever.

This book is a dying promise kept between my dad and my dear Aunt Kelley to keep his perspective alive. It's her chosen medium as a gift to us and I'm so honored to have written the forward to this effort.

My dad wanted us to engage in life, to see the small things, to work together and earn our place on this planet. I know he's up there laughing at all of us most of the time. And I can only imagine the deep welcoming hugs of those I love who will be waiting for me on the other side. But until then, I will rely on the *tribe of characters (whom I love)* that my dad assembled for us to thrive.

This project also benefits the research efforts of finding a cure for melanoma.....and **please, please wear sunscreen, daily.**

Jessica Weems | 2018

"One's destination is never a place but
rather a new way of looking at things."
—HENRY MILLER

His cookies—especially his coveted signature chocolate chip—and his passion (often disguised as temper) were legendary. He was an unofficial master debater, a five star prize bestowed on him that I personally sanctioned. **Secretly, I admired this about him no matter how much frustration it brought up.** He fell hard and swift on one side of an issue and fought for consensus using a variety of tools ranging from charm to insidious obstinacy. What made him wildly successful also made him sometimes hard to be around. What made him thrive also made him irritating. His tenacity was dogged and unyielding—his creativity and inventiveness equally so.

He made his own homemade cheese and included curry and insanely hot peppers in way too many dishes, even eggs. He wore the same pair of US flag boxers on airplanes because if he went down, he wanted the world to know that he was a proud American. He planned the most elaborate and heartwarming traditions and delivered them with such stunning attention to detail that the receivers never doubted for a moment just how loved they were. He was also just past his 42nd year and dying of malignant brain tumors—12 to be exact— the result of metastasized melanoma which rather rapidly spread throughout his entire body.

When the phone rang in the middle of the night, I braced myself for hard news only to hear his chuckling voice on the other end say, "I forgot to tell you one crucial ingredient for my cookies."

"What is it?" I asked.

"Baking soda. How I forgot to tell you to add 1-1/2 teaspoons of baking soda, I'll never know. Let's blame it on the brain tumors but it is absolutely essential to success. I couldn't sleep until I told you. Goodnight."

We weren't particularly close in any traditional sense, David and I. We didn't see each other with any regularity and our phone contact was usually connected to the times he'd answer the line before handing off to his wife, Nicola. David and I were necessary in each others' lives only by the fact that I am his daughters' godmother and his wife's "go-to." When I thought of him, it was mostly in regards to his role as husband and father to a few people in my life I found essential. When I picked up the phone to dial him directly it was usually to discuss some obscure cooking or professional question.

What we did share was a healthy allowance for each other based on our history, our begrudging respect for each others ideas, the people we both loved and a shared passion for all things culinary (he ran epicurean circles around me).

We didn't go about solving problems the same way or have the same life outlook. We did share a few child-raising tips and tools though his iron fisted consequence-by-fire style was in stark contrast to my no-spanking, can't-we-all-just-love credo.

In the early years, we sometimes gently sparred over the belief in miracles or lack thereof. We debated over political points, even if we secretly agreed. He railed, I listened with admittedly smug-like attention, smirked and asked for another glass of red wine which he was happy to deliver but not before a full recitation of grape content, region of origin, tasting notes and a palate testing demonstration. **Nothing was simple with this man and I secretly loved his personal standards even when I rolled my eyes.**

We had a fleeting few philosophical discussions over the years, mostly after a few drinks and always ending up in laughter at our combined absurdity and staunch assuredness. We pushed each others hot buttons and dug in our heels. We also had a couple of epic personal arguments usually brought on by disappointment in each other. And trust me when I acknowledge that these did not bring out the traits either of us would like to be remembered for. It was an unusual friendship forged on proximity not necessarily choice and never one in which I ever expected to deliver such a radical shift of my own perspective.

The truth is that this mans dying process profoundly changed me, my outlook and approach to life. Forever. It shifted how I was willing to spend my hours. It changed the way I serve others. It helped me examine distasteful things about myself and ask some tough internal questions that I had obviously been avoiding.

The seeds of this change were planted in only four simple Sunday night phone calls. I had just shared stories about him over margaritas and for the first time, the realization of what the consequence looked like for his stage of melanoma came into sharp focus. Returning home from dinner, I reached out just to hear his voice and check on their day. I had a sudden urgency to say something which might bring him peace.

My call caught him at the perfect time, he remarked. He'd spent the day with his family and was feeling strong. "And, as Godmother" he said, "I have something I want to talk to you about."

Completely out of character with me, he immediately demanded that I list three things for which I was grateful. To keep the conversation lighthearted and distracting so as not to go anywhere near the irreconcilable concept I had of dying or death, I attempted to steer the mood and enthusiastically listed off queso, margaritas and homemade tortillas. He didn't miss a beat and said, "Yeah, those really are some of the best things in life but what I'm really wanting you to examine are aspects in your world that you have great appreciation and gratitude for—the people you love, your faith, the opportunities you've enjoyed and excelled at, dinner conversations which have resonated or any rituals or traditions you look forward to."

Silence.

This was not at all how our conversations usually evolved. These were not topics of discussion we required of each other. He had never shared any kind of major spiritual proclivity with me. I knew he was meeting regularly with a local pastor who he'd put on the hot seat and who had accepted the honor of rapid-fire questions with grace and humor; two traits David greatly admired. I knew around the house he was talking about angels and salvation and details of messages regarding his time left that he shouldn't have "known." And even though I had a strong belief in spirituality, God and certainly angels, I somehow assigned his enlightened chatter to the brain tumors and the process of dying. Real charitable of me, I know.

Sure, we danced around Easter egg hunts and Christmas traditions but those lent themselves more to customs and the chance to try new recipes rather than any kind of doctrinal teaching lessons. His request and silent patience made me squirmy and I tried again to bring the conversation back around to him and deflect any kind of deep thoughts or anything which might make me cry or make him uncomfortable. I didn't know how to get below the surface of our lovingly adversarial pattern. I didn't know if I wanted to. Instinctively, I somehow knew that this was a genie which could not be forced back into her bottle once coaxed out.

I also recognized this, profoundly, as a wake-up call.

There were some fundamental foundations in place in my life that leaned more toward the familiar, safe and tidy rather than the true, connected and authentic. There was a sense of where everything fit at that point and I was not wanting to examine any of them too closely. I had learned to navigate the order of the life I had helped shape even if it had seemingly been constructed from a checklist one would find online under the search terms of "societal expectations." David refused to let me off the hook and once again encouraged I state aloud that for which I was grateful.

"Are you going all sermon-on-the-mount" with me?" I asked while just trying to buy additional time.

"Yes, I am, actually," he said. "I'm waiting."

And he did without another word. I paused for an unbelievably uncomfortable interval. I took a deep breath. I delivered. And I have never been the same.

For the next four Sundays, I called him and Nicola on the way home from dinner. The first week after our initial conversation, I found myself hyper aware and unsettled. I woke earlier than normal to journal. I was restless and distracted. I would then shift to quiet and stillness. I slowed down. I listened better. I learned to look and see. I heard what people were saying instead of what I thought they were meaning. I watched for extraordinary and simple examples of unity, of connection. I looked for and recognized teamwork—professionally, personally and in the interaction of strangers. I watched kids at play. I noticed dogs and their owners. I counted exactly how many people I crossed paths with in a day. I became enamored and emboldened by the responsibility and chance I might have to connect with perfect strangers even on a small level. I became incredibly present, perhaps for the first time ever.

He knew he was dying. The fact that he had shared his signature cookie recipe was all the proof I needed to accept the crushing fact, myself. Here was a manly man who could build absolutely anything he conceived of. He had three young children he adored, a beautiful wife he loved who it thrilled him to intellectually spar and spoon with in equal measure. He possessed more than his fair share of creativity in life, in cooking, and in business than anyone should be allowed. He was loud, abrasive, head-strong, gruff, boisterous and a soon-to-be-angel himself.

By the fifth Sunday, he passed and I was at a complete loss as to what to do with that weeks worth of collected gratefulness. I had the list dutifully ready and by this time, reciting it was much more than a requirement, it was pure joy. It was a delightful new way of being.

Per Sunday night tradition, I had two margaritas and decided that I'd pay homage through social media to his life and the lessons it provided as a "margarita-fueled shout-out." I knew if I didn't give it some levity, I would have to brace myself to receive a heavenly eye-roll and perhaps a thunderbolt or two zeroed in on my temple. It was meant for no one and everyone at the same time. Through no plan of any kind, I continued to show up every Sunday night and leave my gratefulness as a tiny gift to that curmudgeon of an angel. One post has turned into a decade of observance, insight and tiny moment collecting. These mini mantras have become crucial steps in fully outlining and clarifying my personal guideposts even at an age by which I considered I should have had these things figured out and firmly in place—turns out I didn't. These borrowed wisdoms and collected beauty are a simple documentation of a human being becoming fully awake.

I find great humor in the fact that a self-admitted surly hard-candied shell (with an admittedly sweet center) of a man taught me presence. **His death, but more so, his life, reminded me that this is just what well-lived looks like—the ultimate paradox.** It looks like overwhelming personal failure, it also resembles sweet victory. It looks like accomplishment and it also mimics a messy situation turned around. It looks like never giving up and it also reminds us that sometimes letting go is the gift. It's a commitment to taking great care of ones' tiny little corner of the world and reaching out to those who might benefit from our discoveries. It is community and the realization that we are not alone. It is complex and it is so very simple.

When he left, I truly believe he did so with the unquestionable knowledge that when we expect to find them, we discover *beauty* and *unity* and *connection*. And in that expectation, we find our true joy. I believe he left knowing that nothing else matters.

Outlined within, are 75 collected and random journal prompts of borrowed wisdom and collected beauty. Use them how you see fit. What I've discovered through this process is that no two people read them the same…and I find that incredibly enchanting.

What has delighted me in the last decade are the stories the shout-outs have prompted people to privately share. I am so grateful for the connections I would never have known without this labor of love. If you're inclined, please drop me a line at kelleyrosenyc@gmail.com.

During our last conversation, David signed off with three last demands, " …expect to find good and just keep it in motion. Make sure Nic and the kids are okay. And don't forget to add 1-1/2 teaspoon of baking soda to my cookie recipe… and yes, you can share it now."

THE CURMUDGEON ANGEL'S COOKIES

3 CUPS OF FLOUR
1 1/2 TEASPOON BAKING SODA
1 1/2 TEASPOON SALT
2 STICKS UNSALTED BUTTER (MELTED)
1 1/2 CUPS PACKED BROWN SUGAR
1 CUP GRANULATED SUGAR
3 LARGE EGGS (ROOM TEMPERATURE)
1 1/2 TEASPOONS VANILLA
2 1/2 CUPS DARK CHOCOLATE CHOCOLATE CHIPS

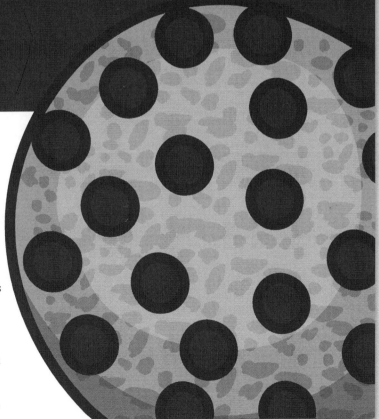

Combine dry ingredients and set aside.

Blend sugars, eggs, vanilla and butter on medium speed then slowly add in sifted dry ingredients.

Bake at 375 for 11 - 12 minutes (watch closely). Do not overbake. Cookies should be slightly crisp on outside and chewy in the middle. Will flatten during cooling. Make sure they are served on a pretty plate with a glass of chilled whole milk. He would like that touch.

JOURNALS ARE AMAZING TOOLS BUT THE REAL MAGIC LIES WITH HOW ONE APPLIES THE REVELATIONS OF THEIR CONTENT

SET IT IN MOTION

No. ONE

…to the vitality and enduring enthusiasm of a shared plan; to massaging into the grooves of a busy life that which you are most curious about; and to the moment when the *bittersweet* leans heavily in the direction of *sweet*. May you rearrange the pieces that have shown up today into something pleasing and yours.

No. TWO

...to the swiftness by which happiness can arrive from within; to the
absolute privilege of maternal shepherding—be it from birth of a child or idea;
and to the unbridled confidence of country dogs. May *you-shaped*
genius find you today and be passed along for us all to enjoy.

No. THREE

…to experiencing the unfolding of magic when one doesn't give up; to the vibrant bounce of a connected conversation; and to recognizing that the things you doodled in the margins long, long ago were clues. Today, may a still moment of thankfulness wash over you like an unexpected waterfall.

No. FOUR

...to embracing the winds of change by choosing an extraordinary kite to fly; to the messiness between the smiles; and to beauty from the ashes. May you allow for all the different shapes and sounds of happy today.

_____

_____

_____

_____

_____

_____

_____

_____

_____

_____

_____

_____

_____

_____

_____

_____

No. FIVE

…to the pursuit of life badges you actually want; to adopting a personal manifesto which contains grit and good; and to filling in the gap between reality and a dream. May anyone rebuilding today find strength and community to do so with linked arms and satisfied hearts.

WATCHING THE NURTURED BLOSSOM INTO THE NURTURER

IS THE CIRCLE OF LIFE

No. SIX

...to tight hugs you don't want to release; to the tribe who steps in to walk beside us in times of challenge; and to understanding that the creativity given to us is not ours to keep but must be passed along. May you feel lit from within at some point today and feel inclined to pay the love forward.

No. SEVEN

…to love eclipsing all hate no matter which flag you fly; to
remembering and honoring our individual responsibility to
that effort; and to the story you're living—may it be one you're proud
of and eager to greet each day. May today expose a different
perspective which delights, informs and inspires.

No. EIGHT

… to the feeling of the biggest stretch after a long and dormant
slumber; to the splendor found in the stillness; and to the discovery
along the way….to anything. May you make a valiant run
at the cherry on top today.

No. NINE

...to the seasons we pass through—the ones which both inform and inspire; to suspending the stories we assign those we truly know very little about; and to that which prompts us to climb down a ladder and choose another if what we find at the top strays from that which we sense is the way forward. May an unexpected burst of joy envelop you at some point today.

No. TEN

…to those who show up and reflect your happy right back at you; to the way a heartbeat raises and hands begin moving when a really great idea or inspiration sneaks up on you; and to recognizing the truth—yours. May the tightest and most sincere hug find you today.

ACTING ON DREAMS
DELAYED IS EVERYTHING

MOMENTUM IS CONTAGIOUS

No. ELEVEN

…to adventuring with a favorite human; to the echo of ones own laughter; and to the ripples a good idea generates. May you find yourself at some point today, imagining what the very best version of yourself might think like.

No. TWELVE

…to that which you hold mandatory in your life; to the long way around and enjoying the trip; and to creating something from that pulse inside. May your sense of exhilaration and adventure steer you today.

No. THIRTEEN

…to keeping good things in motion and seeing what kind of magic ensues; to dreaming up the most impossible thing you could ever imagine that might thrill you and watching it unfold; and to understanding there is PLENTY… and passing what you might along. May you find yourself on the cool side of synchronicity today.

No. FOURTEEN

...to experiences which threaten to break ones smile muscles; to those indelible moments of decisiveness when good-natured defiance gurgles up and one recognizes that fear has become fuel; and to the harmony and sway of well-matched personalities. May you say, YES! to something today... very quickly...and then figure out how.

No. FIFTEEN

...to respect—earning it and giving it; to recognizing that the way you're looking is the way you're heading; and to courting happy. May you usher in the new day with a hint-o-mischief.

BESTING OURSELVES

IS A LIFELONG PURSUIT

No. SIXTEEN

…to the resonance of truth; to chasing impulse with a big smile and
an even bigger net; and to the expectation of expansion. Today,
may you move a personal bar you've been staring at up a notch just because
you're curious to see if you can.

No. SEVENTEEN

...to those who become family without any shared bloodline; to the ones who push you way past personal goals with inspiration and joy; and to the ones who gently pick you up when you hit a wall at warp speed and urge you on. May a kind glance from a stranger pass through your life today.

No. EIGHTEEN

…to not underestimating the value of ones preferences; to the
personal rituals which entice creation and expansion; and
to courting the intimate over the grandiose.
May a smile-which-won't-quit be yours today.

No. NINETEEN

…to joy without condition; to embracing the whirlwind that accompanies radical change; and to the bounce a beautiful day puts in ones' step. May you set in motion today that which you've hesitated on for far too long.

No. TWENTY

…to reverence for the parents—yours, mine and theirs; to lessons observed at the dog park; and to loading your own personal ark with only that which matters….and leaving the rest behind. May a chance encounter today leave you with a warm center.

THE CHOIR IN OUR HEAD LIKES ALL TYPES OF MUSIC

ALLOW YOURSELF TO BE MULTI-PASSIONATE

No. TWENTY-ONE

…to the conviction of your dreams (no matter how sky high they seem); to the
sovereignty of self expression; and to releasing all
illusions of control (without panic). May you make room for a
variety of love to flood your life today.

No. TWENTY TWO

…to the chaos of creativity; to the irradiation of love which long walks stimulate; and to the wisdom of youth (it's there and always was). May you catch a glimpse of a tiny thoughtful act today.

No. TWENTY THREE

...to the Elysian quality of a summer day in the city; to the illumination of oneself that true friendship inspires; and to eschewing the "*shoulds*" for the "*coulds*." May an overheard comment today shift a well-worn pattern of thought.

No. TWENTY FOUR

...to all the maybes one is willing to consider; to the irrelevancy of excuses; and to reminding yourself on a daily basis what you once dreamed of. May the tiniest of detail make the mightiest of difference today.

No. TWENTY FIVE

…to loosening the grip on that which was not meant for us; to stepping
into adventure all hands-up rollercoaster-style; and to a treasure hunt
way of life. May you wish for yourself today one of the things you
dream for someone you love.

TAILWINDS ARRIVE
IN MANY FORMS

EXPECT THEM

No. TWENTY SIX

...to the clarity of conviction; to a carefully examined measure of success; and to embracing the unexpected with a tight hug and wry grin. May you discover a new way to create belonging today.

No. TWENTY SEVEN

…to beauty that has nothing whatsoever to do with vanity; to "giving ledges/boxes/stations" and other ways in which love is passed along; and to understanding that unfulfilled potential is simply an invitation to rise. May you *pause and hear* and *stop and see* at least once today.

No. TWENTY EIGHT

...to the surrender of the adventure; to the inherent salve in the words of
a true friend; and to those who gently remind us to look where
we're going....ahead. May you pay forward today, one kindness
shown to you at some point in your life.

No. TWENTY NINE

…to the highly individualistic interpretation of comfort and joy;
to the deceptive nature of doubt; and to green grass—yours. May a hand you
hold today be steady and strong.

No. THIRTY

...to weighing if the juice is worth the squeeze; to the magic of the afterthoughts and marginalia; and to the refusal to shrug off the awareness once it finds you. May you feel compelled to reach for something today you feel might be just beyond your place of comfort.

SCRAPS OF BEAUTY CAN BE SEWN TOGETHER WITH STAGGERING RESULTS

COLLECT THEM

No. THIRTY ONE

…to those who let go before you're ready, may you send them love; to heeding the mighty whisper calling you to share your brand of genius; and to the beautiful paralyzing fear which visits right before transformation. Today, may you turn in the direction of the call.

No. THIRTY TWO

...to joy as a driving force; to those who understand that the most authentic life is how the world is best served; and to staying the course. May you tap into a vein of tenacity today to fulfill something important.

No. THIRTY THREE

…to unplugging and looking up; to simple words backed by complex actions; and to the questions we ask ourselves and the answers we give. May a tiny crack of light penetrate your biggest challenge today.

_____

_____

_____

_____

_____

_____

_____

_____

_____

_____

_____

_____

_____

_____

_____

_____

_____

_____

No. THIRTY FOUR

…to the recognition and respect for the beauty of the complex (humans and dreams); to repeating as many times as we possibly must that we are one, we are one, we are one, we are one, we are one; and to just sittin' and holdin' when there's nothing we can do to "fix" it. May you pass along what you knew in your most peaceful moment today.

No. THIRTY FIVE

… to the absolute privilege of maternal shepherding—be it from the birth of a child or an idea; to action on dreams delayed ; and to the unbridled confidence of country dogs. May you-shaped genius find you today and be passed along for us all to enjoy.

DECIDE WHO RIDES IN YOUR CANOE

IT MATTERS

No. THIRTY SIX

...to the love behind the frankness some offer; to becoming
an enthusiast...of anything; and to old souls which circle back
around into ones life with priceless vigor and grace. May you begin
to heed the calling of a particular goal today.

No. THIRTY SEVEN

…to the charmingly naive steps it takes to be a beginner; to the cadence of a long walk when inspiration strikes; and to those who leave joy and connection, wisdom and love in their wake. May you receive a deep and restorative neck scrunch today.

No. THIRTY EIGHT

…to the unifying magic which occurs when you face down challenges together; to emulating those whom you admire; and to adjusting your gaze and grip on that which does not serve or uplift. May your sweater weather perspective have bounce today.

No. THIRTY NINE

…to "good enough" not being a personal standard you adopt; to listening and being heard; and to your words flowing in the way of your intentions in every situation. May you stretch yourself today because you know you have it in you and that's the way you want to show up.

No. FORTY

…to the character-building opportunities the chop and churn unchartered waters provide; to embracing the truths which emerge when one takes a long and introspective look inside; and to the siren song of that thing you'll almost allow yourself to dream. May the new season bring you something pleasant you have never known….and may it be delightful.

SOMETIMES THE GREATEST ACT OF LOVE IS LETTING GO

BUT IT HURTS LIKE A THOUSAND
CAMELS RUNNING ROUGHSHOD
OVER YOUR HEART

No. FORTY ONE

…to the smells of Sunday; to beauty that has a lot more to do with spirit rather than artifice; and to delightful distractions which catch us in the midst of focus and work to sharpen rather than blur the lines.
May your mischief hat get the most wear today.

No. FORTY TWO

…to the possibility of encountering enchanting humans around every corner; to the quickening heartbeat at the recognition of adventure; and to remembering what you seek and why you do so. May a cherished memory cross your mind today.

No. FORTY THREE

…to the courage to step into another version of yourself—not false, just new;
to never allowing your truth to be eclipsed by someone else's agenda;
and to the well-timed nudge that arrives from the unlikeliest of sources. May the
winds of change blow in something delightful for you today.

No. FORTY FOUR

…to allowing contradictory truths to live side-by-side; to charging onward all Joan of Arc style; and to allowing the jagged edges of the family tree to still be beautiful. May what you ask be given (and may you be grateful).

No. FORTY FIVE

...to the contagious nature of ardor; to the intersection of *what if* and *chance*; and to personal hallmarks of joy. May a perfect stranger share a perspective you can't stop thinking about today.

PERSONAL MOJO IS AN INSIDE JOB

AN ESSENTIAL FOUNDATION

No. FORTY SIX

...to the futility of watering plastic flowers; to seeing your ship and being willing to swim out to meet it; and to viewing criticism as a gift rather than a whip. May you give yourself a *high five* and *round of applause* today.

No. FORTY SEVEN

…to the anchoring few who will hold your kite string as you explore what you must; to running directly toward those who demand your best; and to the peculiarly satisfying tiny shared experiences. May the season of change ignite more than the firewood.

No. FORTY EIGHT

...to the audacity of believing it's possible; to tailwinds which arrive in many forms; and to stolen moments you didn't see coming. May someone share something with resonates and mimics the sound of love for you today today.

No. FORTY NINE

...to the discerning curation of ones' day (and those in it); to the personal inventory of that which matters; and to the sobering force of Mother Nature (may we respect Her always). May community be a verb today.

HANDWRITTEN LETTERS & DEEP HUGS

TWO OF THE GREATEST EFFORTS OF ALL

No. FIFTY

...to holding onto that which serves our greatest purpose; to the imprint
you wish to leave on others, this world; and to reminding those who
may feel alone that they are not. May a quiet space today reveal
an extraordinarily simple revelation.

No. FIFTY ONE

…to meeting people where they are and loving them hard; to the connectivity of inside humor; and to the responsibility of passing along the grace we have been extended. May you ensure someone feels they belong today.

No. FIFTY TWO

…to understanding that grace is contagious; to those who encourage without restraint; and to those who resist being loved (long and tight hugs anyway). May you leave light on your path today.

_____

_____

_____

_____

_____

_____

_____

_____

_____

_____

_____

_____

_____

_____

_____

_____

No. FIFTY THREE

…to the charm of the mystery; to the auspicious and fruitful nature of an occasional rainy Sunday; and to the beautiful exchange of giving and receiving. May kindness be thrown out like parade candy in your direction today….and may some hit you.

NOTABLE PEOPLE

LOVE THEM UP COMPLETELY.
BE ONE.

No. FIFTY FOUR

…to those who passed through and left something worthy and unexpected; to those who understand that comparison robs one of an authentic effort; and to those who give what they most could use and do so without the expectation of reciprocity. May you see someone very familiar in a new and brilliant light today.

No. FIFTY FIVE

…to those who string a beautiful life together pearl-by-pearl; to finding your voice and holding steady; and to those who create and share without restraint. May you visit the place today just outside your personal comfort zone and may you go there often.

THE MESSY AND THE SAD STILL INFORM.

IF YOU ALLOW IT

No. FIFTY SIX

…to rocking shared perspectives and making collaboration King; to those who reflect light back onto everyone with whom they cross paths; and to those who lead with strategic play instead of buttoned-up seriousness. May you find a creative solution to a serious subject today.

NO. FIFTY SEVEN

...to the questions we ask ourselves and the answers we give; to common goals with divergent paths (and respect for both); and to blind and absolute faith in ourselves, our futures, our path. May you put something out into the world today just for the sake of sharing what's inside.

No. FIFTY EIGHT

…to pushing through self-censorship; to progress and momentum (whatever that looks like for you); and to five small steps toward an objective every single day. May the gift at the end of your efforts be something you're proud to share —a true reflection of what you came to leave.

No. FIFTY NINE

...to tradition steeped in history which unites and excites; to great escapes (even if from the comfort of your favorite armchair); and to the essential nature of adult swim time. May you bring as much creativity to your partnership as you do to your favorite pastime.

No. SIXTY

…to the fact that a cookie sometimes IS the answer (enjoy it); to the challenges only girlfriends can make better; and to a S-L-O-W dinner with someone who could care less what time it is. May your presence today be given freely and joyfully.

YOUR CHILDREN SHOULD SEE
YOU PROUD OF YOURSELF

FOR ANYTHING

No. SIXTY ONE

…to anticipation in every form; to the delightful distractions you'll laugh at in your most private moments; and to making the mundane an adventure. May you regularly seek to delight those around you on simple Tuesday nights. Or Thursdays. Or any day of the week.

No. SIXTY TWO

…to the invisible power of wearing pretty panties even if you're the only one who sees them; to wholeheartedly stepping into whatever your version of *life balance* looks like, feels like; and to those who demand the best *from* and want the best *for* you. May you happen upon a beautiful memory today.

No. SIXTY THREE

…to those who change lives without expectation; to those who don't hesitate to raise their hand when needs arise; and to the restorative nature of the occasional solo escape. May an opportunity to *go* find you today.

No. SIXTY FOUR

…to the space between thought and action (may it be short); to that which you can't understand but choose to respect; and to those you would invite onto your park blanket. May clarity and self-awareness be yours today.

_____

_____

_____

_____

_____

_____

_____

_____

_____

_____

_____

_____

_____

_____

_____

_____

_____

_____

No. SIXTY FIVE

...to allowing pain and confusion to live alongside love; to understanding the growth potential in them all; and to healing through giving and creating. May the challenges you face leave blessings in their place.

_____

_____

_____

_____

_____

_____

_____

_____

_____

_____

_____

_____

_____

_____

_____

_____

_____

_____

JUST LIKE MARY POPPINS' MAGIC BAG, YOU CARRY WITH YOU EVERYTHING YOU'D EVER NEED TO CREATE CONNECTION AND BELONGING.

TRUST IT

No. SIXTY SIX

...to choice and the responsibility of it; to kindness when least expected; and to the trusting your internal lighthouse—it always knows the way. May you call someone today who would absolutely love to hear your voice.

No. SIXTY SEVEN

...to the potential which white space holds—a canvas, a piece of
paper, a blinking screen, an empty room; to filling it;
and to sharing it with someone. May today be all about expression.

No. SIXTY EIGHT

…to an abundant brain; to a receptive brain; and to using them both.
May they collide today in a beautiful way.

No. SIXTY NINE

…to expertly navigated challenges; to the use of unexpected charm (surprise someone); and to being interested —in them, in that. May you unplug today and be really present with someone who could use some face time.

No. SEVENTY

…to choosing love over fear, love over fear, love over fear—every time;
to flinging yourself and your gifts into an effort so much bigger than you; and
to paying forward graces which have been extended in your direction. May you
choose someone to *lovebomb* today.

WE WON'T TASTE GOOD TO EVERYONE

YOU DO YOU, ANYWAY

No. SEVENTY ONE

...to compelling stories and those who share them with us; to understanding
that life is also really long and who's in it with you REALLY matters;
and to glimpses of humans doing extraordinary things with their time.
May you take a micro-step toward a long forgotten objective today.

NO. SEVENTY TWO

...to right brain ideas and left brain tactics; to personal manifestos which
beat inside your chest; and to stepping toward that which
intrigues and intimidates in equal measure (you're on to something).
May you scare yourself a little today and act.

No. SEVENTY THREE

…to those single glances where whole paragraphs are exchanged; to seemingly mundane moments which offer a glimpse of the extraordinary; and to besting ourselves (and repeating the process regularly). May you laugh at your hesitation today.

No. SEVENTY FOUR

...to welcoming the beginner brain at any season of life; to puppy snuggles as therapy; and to the lessons our children teach US.
May you soak up the love surrounding you like a sponge today.

No. SEVENTY FIVE

…to the art of a well-executed hug; to rainy days and roaring fires; and to those who understand that this is our one shot — to keep good in motion is entirely the point of this life journey. May you choose to participate with every fiber of your being.

ACKNOWLEDGMENTS

To the tribe of souls it took to bring these decade-long
spontaneous blurts of gratitude to print.

Special thanks to Nicola Weems who
encouraged this project all the way through.
And to Jessica Weems who shared so much.

To Gladys Tynes, my beloved Senior English teacher, who
made story and expression come to life and
taught me the importance of five paragraph themes.

And to Cindy Stanley for the cover art.

ABOUT THE AUTHOR | KELLEY ROSE

Kelley Rose is a proud Texan living a dream delayed in NYC.
She began collecting these Sunday Night Margarita-Fueled Shout-Outs
a decade ago in an attempt to process loss—what she discovered is that
the habit of documenting them has become an
essential discipline in processing life.

Her next project is an online brand created as a resource for
those attempting to define, *What's Next?*.

Second Bloom is a call-to-action
for those looking to reimagine life.

www.secondbloomlife.com